What Do You Like to Eat?

Written by Josephine Selwyn

Picture Dictionary

apple

bread

marshmallows

Read the picture dictionary. You will find these words in the book.

popcorn

turkey

watermelon

We like this food.

apple

We like this food.

turkey

We like this food.

popcorn

We like this food.

bread

We like this food.

watermelon

We like this food.

marshmallows

Activity Page

1. Rewrite the book with different foods.

2. Write the new dictionary words.

3. Draw matching pictures.

Do you know the dictionary words?

badge
POLICE

Look at me.
I am a firefighter.

helmet

Look at me.
I am a doctor.

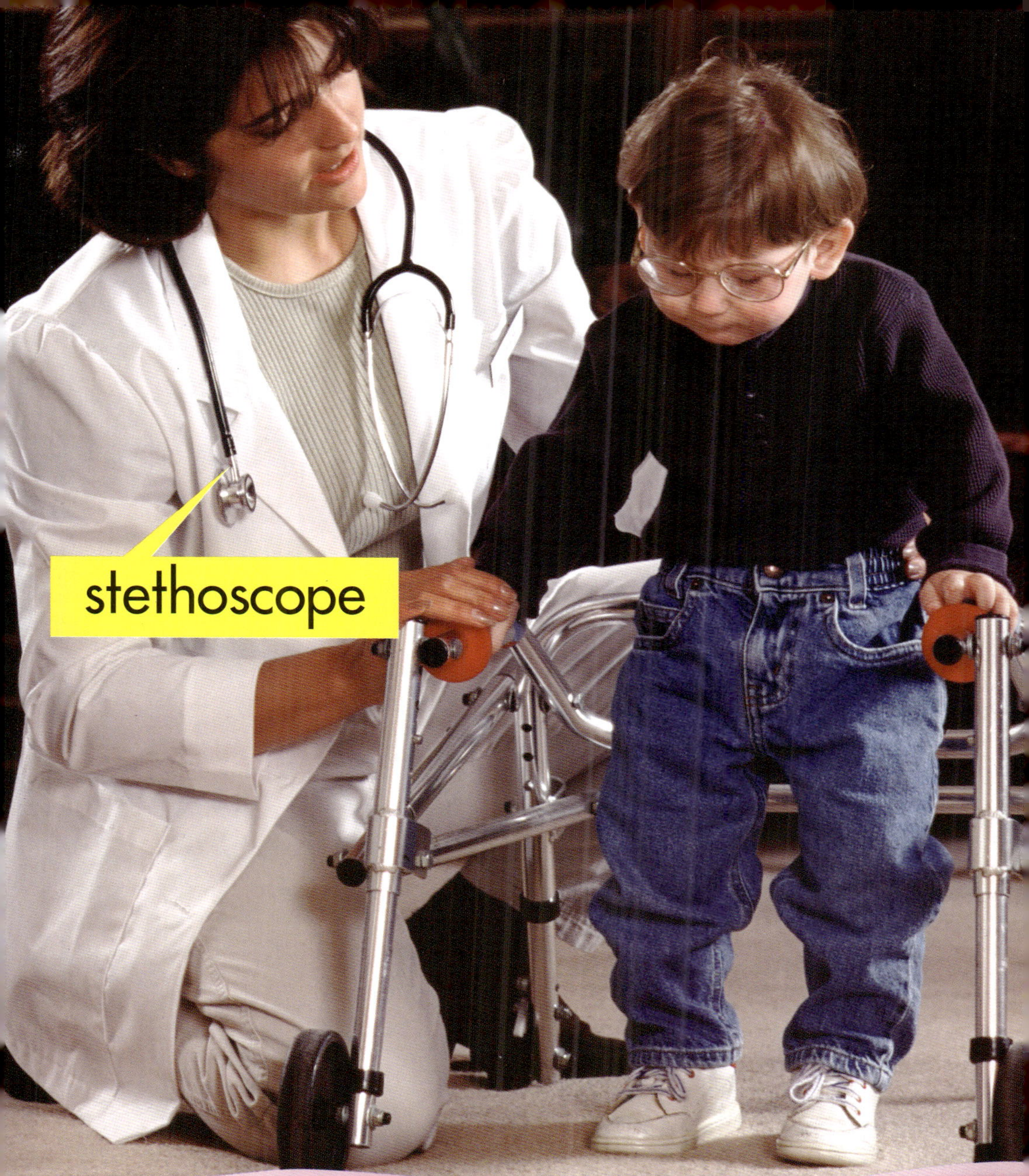
stethoscope

Look at me.
I am a dentist.

toothbrush

Look at me.
I am a baker.

hat

Look at me.
I am a teacher.

board
Classroom
1) No fighting
Be polite to each other.
7) One person talking at a time.
8) No teasing.

Activity Page

1. Draw a police car.
2. Draw a police officer sitting in the car.
3. Write a speech balloon: I am a police officer.

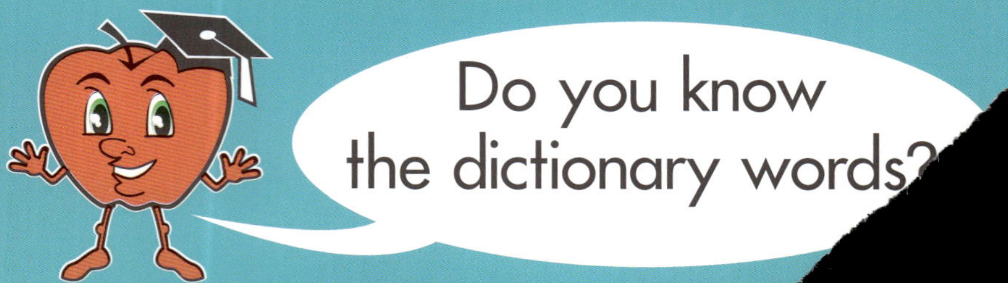

Jobs People Do

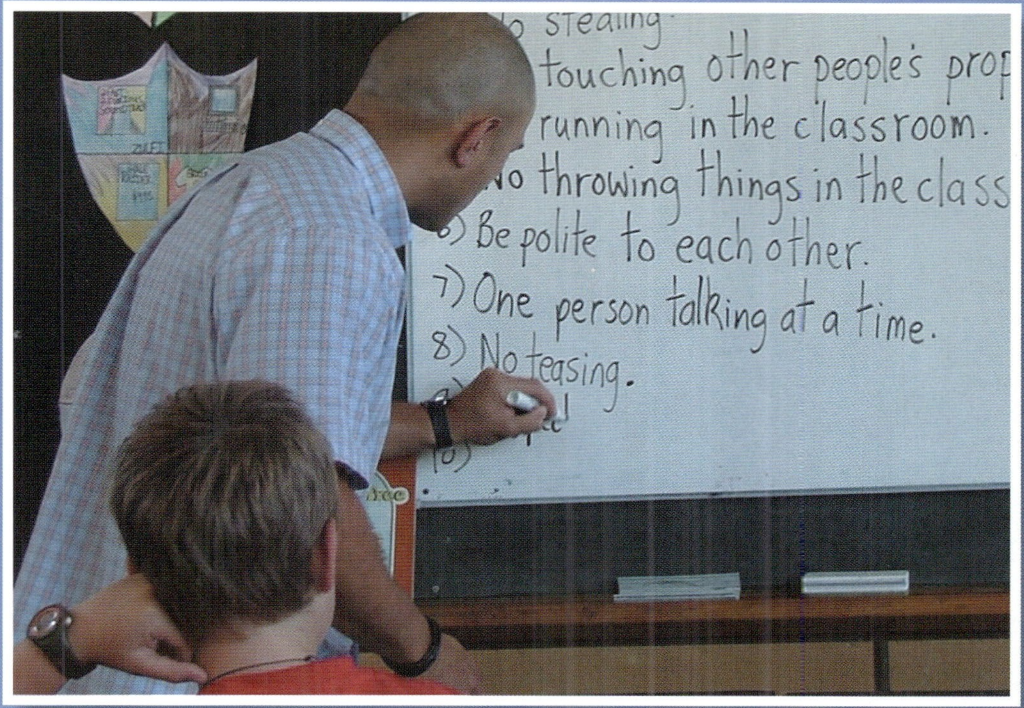

Written by Josephine Selwyn

Picture Dictionary

baker

dentist

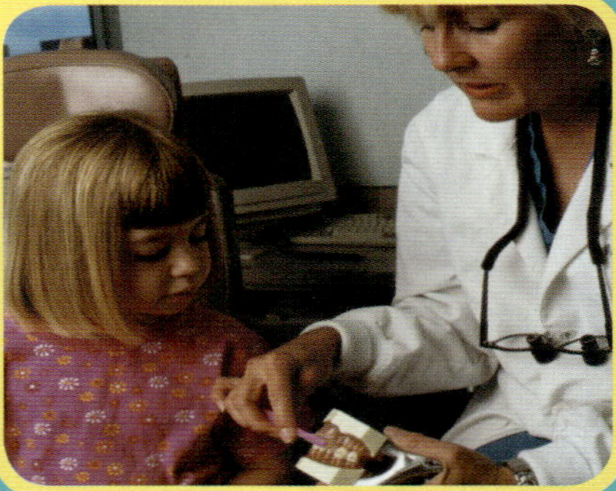

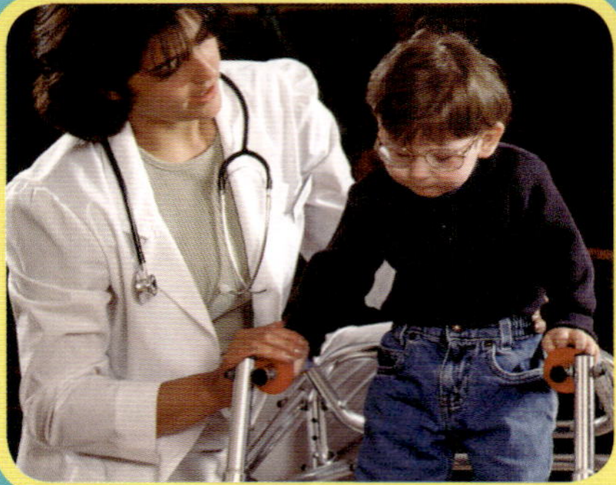

doctor

Read the picture dictionary. You will find these words in the book.

firefighter

police officer

teacher

Look at me.
I am a police officer.